Women
Pray

Women Pray

Edited by

Karen L. Roller

THE PILGRIM PRESS
New York

Library of Congress Cataloging-in-Publication Data

Women pray.

    1. Women—Prayer-books and devotions—English.
I. Roller, Karen L., 1958-
BV283.W6W66   1986   242'.643   86–15117
ISBN 0-8298-0737-3 (pbk.)

The Pilgrim Press, 132 West 31 Street, New York, New
York 10001

Contents

Introduction

Women Pray is the realization of a small but persistent dream—to find a way for women to share their prayers as gifts to one another and the larger faith community. These prayers by women have been collected in response to a request from the United Church of Christ Coordinating Center for Women in Church and Society. We gratefully acknowledge the gifts of Karen Roller, editor, and of all the women who shared our dream and offered their prayers.

Women pray in worship and at their kitchen tables; they pray at communion and over a sack lunch; they pray over their children and for all the world's children.

Women pray for other women, for justice, for peace, and for patience to forgive those who would deny justice and peace in our world.

Women pray alone, in silence; and with voices hushed or strong. They lift up their prayers with other women; when women gather, be it two or three, or a thousand, they gather in prayer.

Women pray in joy and celebration. They pray in pain and anguish, longing only for the healing of God's grace.

Women's prayers celebrate the seasons of women's lives; from the innocent trusting prayers of childhood to the awakening prayers of youth and the searching prayers of maturing years; the compassionate prayers of wisdom and the sometimes lonely prayers of old age.

We offer all these prayers for use in your own times of joy and sorrow; use them freely as you pray, alone or with others. Accept each of them as the gift of another woman, letting her prayer become your own, sharing each other's gifts as women pray.

Marilyn M. Breitling, Executive
Coordinating Center for Women
in Church and Society

Women Together

Opening Words

Centering

A Morning Prayer

OPENING WORDS

In the name of the Creator who gathers us
   Let God's name be praised
In the name of Jesus who frees us
   Let God's name be praised
In the name of the Spirit who sustains us
   Let God's name be praised.

Who are we?
   We are people who have come to learn.
   We are people who can teach each other.
   We are different.
   We are the same.
   We are the people of God.
   We are women of the church.

Why are we here?
   To worship, to sing in joy, to grow and stretch,
   To experience our power, to share our stories and our
      skills,
   To strengthen our leadership in God's church and
   To renew our commitment to struggle for the
   Coming of justice throughout the world.

May God go with us.

Amen.

*—First National Meeting
of United Church of Christ Women*

CENTERING

LEADER: Holy Spirit, renewing energy,
by you, we are born again as daughters of
God; you make us living temples of your
presence, you pray within us prayers too
deep for words.

PEOPLE: **In returning and rest,**
In quietness and confidence shall be our
strength.

LEADER: Be still and know that God is here.

PEOPLE: **Be still and know that God is here.**
Be still and know that God is here.
(People continue chanting together these
words of peace and tranquility, centering
again and again on God's presence in our
own being, and in our midst.)

—Second National Meeting
of United Church of Christ Women

3

A MORNING PRAYER

Spirit of God, whose love for us is surer than the sun's rising, we thank you for gathering us in this time of worship wherein we remember who and whose we are. Here we know that we are yours and one another's—a people called by love to love. We are glad that in prayer we may speak freely, dropping the masks that too often keep us hidden, even from ourselves. Because you cherish us, because you forgive us, we can come to this place and go from this place with renewed confidence for our living and stronger hope for our dying. How good it is to know that you care for us!

Trusting in your care, we offer our concerns to you. We pray for those it is sometimes easiest and sometimes hardest to love—our families and friends, thanking you for the challenges and joys of intimate caring. And we pray for all who are known and unknown to us who are ill or lonely or in any distress. Reach them, we ask, with your strength and peace.

We lift up to you the pain of our planet—its scarred land, its tainted waters, its endangered creatures. Even as we enjoy the fruits of the earth, remind us, Creator God, that you have entrusted your handiwork to us. May we respect all life you have given.

O God, our Liberator, free us from every hesitation to serve you and our neighbors. Even toward our "enemies" give us less hardened hearts and made-up minds. Keep in your care and our awareness all who suffer because we cannot yet live the vision of Shalom in its fullness—those who wander homeless, those who are imprisoned, those who have disappeared, those who have died. May we who are gathered here take up the vision and hasten the day when "the wolf shall lie down with the lamb. . .and the earth shall be filled with the knowledge of God as the waters cover the sea."*

Amen.

—*Ann B. Day*
Holden, Massachusetts

*See Isaiah 11:6, 9.

Woman to Woman

Your Messenger Was a Woman

Know You as Woman

Words of Women

YOUR MESSENGER WAS A WOMAN

O gracious God,
> your messenger was a woman who changed some tired rules and altered a few, feeble notions. She shared your story and led your people with wisdom, helping us to see a vision of new ways.

O gracious God,
> I thank you for sending this woman who was able to plant the seeds of change with integrity.

O God of tenderness,
> you lifted my small daughter's eyes to a pulpit where she could see the smile of a woman. A mother's voice told her about you in everyday words. The mother inside those formal robes squatted down to touch her little hand and ask about her cat.

O God of tenderness,
> you spoke through a mother, and I thank you for sending your message of love with a gentle touch and a calm voice.

O teacher God,
> you sent a role model to the young teenager in the back pew. I watched the young girl's eyes shine when she realized that she had found an adult she could trust and admire.

O teacher God,
>your guidance came from a woman, and I thank you for the images of hope and possibility that she embodied for the young.

O friend God,
>you spoke to me of hurt and healing through this woman, and I leaned back in poignant recognition of our commonality. You gave me an interpreter of your Word and a listener to mine who knew where I'd been.

O friend God,
>you comforted my heart as only a sister could. Through your servant I found generous welcome, warmth, and understanding. I praise you for her supportive presence.

O nurturing God,
>by this woman's example, you filled me with strength and pride, and my soul was released from its usual hesitant frame. From the pulpit or at my kitchen table, your minister spoke of confidence and promise. She reminded me of your help in time of need and your ever-present Spirit.

O nurturing God,
>I thank you for this woman, filled with your empowering Spirit. She valued my mind, my experience, and my compassion and challenged me to be your active servant. She helped me to say "yes" to myself and to you.

O God,
>thank you for sending this woman.

>*—Lilia M. Behr*
>*Brainerd, Minnesota*

KNOW YOU AS WOMAN

Dear God, I sit beside this special person who has lost her breast and I pray somehow she can know you as Woman. As Mother, you have cradled me in my own pain as I seek to comfort her. Would that she knew your femininity! There is a level of breast surgery only another female can understand, as I wish she knew how intimately you, Creator of woman and man, grieve with her. Precious Spirit, your presence in this hurting is so much a reality for me. Touch this wounded sister of my soul in your powerful love, Woman to woman and even greater. *Amen.*

—Dianna Niemann Harris
Ferguson, Missouri

WORDS OF WOMEN

LEADER: Creator God, hear now our prayer of gratitude and thanksgiving for creation *in general*, for *our* creation and for all *creativity*. We ask *(this evening)* that we be helped to celebrate our blessings and re-dedicate our lives. We lift our voices in the *Magnificat* of Mary. Hear these words of women.

PEOPLE: **Our souls magnify the Lord, and our spirits rejoice in God our Savior . . .***

LEADER: That we stand with generations of women who know that the Lord their God is One God; who love the Lord with all their hearts and minds and strength; who established the legacy of Sarah and Deborah and Ruth.

PEOPLE: **Our souls magnify the Lord, and our spirits rejoice in God our Savior . . .**

LEADER: That we share the news with those first women at the tomb, who went forth to proclaim the gospel of Jesus Christ; who served the early Christians with zeal; who were named Mary and Phoebe and Priscilla.

PEOPLE: **Our souls magnify the Lord, and our spirits rejoice in God our Savior . . .**

LEADER: That we can remember those women who shaped the church in cloistered community and civil court; who listened to inner voices and pursued mystical union; who mothered and married the "fathers of the faith"; who loved the church when it was most unlovable.

PEOPLE: **Our souls magnify the Lord, and our spirits rejoice in God our Savior . . .**

LEADER: That we can honor women who defended the reformed faith and supported the reformers; who gave up comforts and family for their convictions; who were sometimes called witches and often became mar-

*See Luke 1:46–47.

tyrs; who arrived in the new world and took new responsibilities.

PEOPLE: **Our souls magnify the Lord, and our spirits rejoice in God our Savior . . .**

LEADER: That we now recall those women who came to this land not on the deck, but in the dark hold of a slave ship; who preserved an African heritage and understood the liberating message of the Christian gospel; who nurtured a church under Jim Crow and Daddy Grace; who know the double jeopardy of being black and female.

PEOPLE: **Our souls magnify the Lord, and our spirits rejoice in God our Savior . . .**

LEADER: That we now listen to those native American sisters whose people were here long before anyone came to this country; who remind us of the interrelated fabric of earth and sky and sea; who know the pain of displacement and betrayal; who have much to share with all women.

PEOPLE: **Our souls magnify the Lord, and our spirits rejoice in God our Savior . . .**

LEADER: That we can read in history of missionaries who heard a call to teach and heal in the name of Jesus; who shared their faith with women and children throughout the world; who exercised authority with charity, if not always wisdom; who widened the horizons and expanded the vision of the church.

PEOPLE: **Our souls magnify the Lord, and our spirits rejoice in God our Savior . . .**

LEADER: That we know also of strong women who

12

stayed at home and worked in groups and churches to change American life; who founded antislavery societies, Sunday schools, peace movements, suffrage organizations, and temperance halls; who saved and raised monies for mission at home and abroad; who were proud of "women's work" and kept the churches going.

PEOPLE: **Our souls magnify the Lord, and our spirits rejoice in God our Savior . . .**

LEADER: That we are enriched by the influx of Pacific and Asian women who bridge the cultural gulf between East and West and raise our global awareness; who come from islands where women have valued tradition; who know the problems of multicultural and multilingual communities in our urban society.

PEOPLE: **Our souls magnify the Lord, and our spirits rejoice in God our Savior . . .**

LEADER: That we are heirs of those women who challenged the status quo and pioneered in new roles; who insisted on a woman's right to preach the gospel, to practice medicine, to defend the law, to hold public office; who refused to let tradition and custom stifle their gifts; who call the church to accept new forms of leadership even today.

PEOPLE: **Our souls magnify the Lord, and our spirits rejoice in God our Savior . . .**

LEADER: That there are women who have worked in the churches as wives of pastors; who, although too often unacclaimed and unnoticed, have given of themselves in a faithful and dedicated ministry.

PEOPLE: **Our souls magnify the Lord, and our spirits rejoice in God our Savior . . .**

LEADER: That we are learning to love those women who are variously called Latino, Hispanic, Chicano, Mexican, and Puerto Rican; who speak Spanish in our church; who know the journeys of employment and the waste of unemployment; who add yet another culture and language to the church.

PEOPLE: **Our souls magnify the Lord, and our spirits rejoice in God our Savior . . .**

LEADER: That we are *all* of these women who seek to serve you, *our* God. We offer this prayer of thanksgiving and gratitude. We are many, and yet we are one. We are bound together as creatures. We are joined together as women. We are members of the church of Jesus Christ. We are empowered for mission because of these women. Thank you, Lord. Thank you, Lord. *Amen.*

—First National Meeting
of United Church of Christ Women

14

Images of God

Forgotten Images

Names of God

Marvelous and Mysterious

FORGOTTEN IMAGES

Dear God of Us All,

They have forgotten you.
They have twisted your images as midwife, as pregnant
   being, as nursing mother, and called you "he" with no
   room for she.
They thought ignoring you would make you disappear.
They claim nexus to a male god without consort or equal.
They desire dominance, justified by a god up there.
They do not understand your Oneness.

Dear God of Us All,

We have forgotten you too.
We have accepted invisibility, yours and ours,
   without a fight.
We mistook our servanthood for slavery.
We forgot ourselves.
We fear your offer of freedom.

Dear God of Us All,

Help us to know that you Are and always Will Be.
Help us to receive your nurturing as strength.
Help us to realize that embracing life can never be en-
   slaving.
Help us to never, ever, forget you again!

—*Lois H. Grace Stovall*
Charlotte, North Carolina

NAMES OF GOD

LEADER: O God, because you are the source of all life and love and being,

PEOPLE: **We call you Creator, . . .**

LEADER: Because we know the history of your presence among your covenanted people and honor their tradition,

PEOPLE: **We call you Lord, . . .**

LEADER: Because our Savior, Jesus Christ, your obedient child, knew you intimately and spoke of you so,

PEOPLE: **We call you Father, . . .**

LEADER: Because you are present in the act of birth and because you shelter, nurture, and care for us,

PEOPLE: **We call you Mother, . . .**

LEADER: Because you hold us up and give us strength and courage when we are weak and in need,

PEOPLE: **We call you Sustainer, . . .**

LEADER: Because we have known you in our pain and suffering,

PEOPLE: **We call you Comforter, . . .**

LEADER: Because beyond pain lies your promise of all things made new,

PEOPLE: **We call you Hope, . . .**

17

LEADER:	Because you are the means of liberation and the way to freedom,
PEOPLE:	**We call you Deliverer, . . .**
LEADER:	Because you have chosen to come among us and share our common lot, making the hard choices, suffering and dying; because you rose victorious, bringing new life,
PEOPLE:	**We call you Redeemer, . . .**
ALL:	**Confident that you will hear, we call upon you with all the names that make you real to us, the names which create an image in our minds and hearts, an image which our souls can understand and touch. And yet, we know that you are more than all of these. Blessing and power, glory and honor be unto you, our God. *Amen.***

*—Second National Meeting
of United Church of Christ Women*

18

MARVELOUS AND MYSTERIOUS

We lift up our hearts, our voices, our eyes unto you, Holy God. In you is our hope and salvation, you who in word and wonder created the heavens, dotting the night skies with moon and stars and the day skies with sun and sumptuous blues, and you who knelt down on the dust of the earth's floor and fashioned us by hand out of clay, lovingly molding us in your hands and designing us in your image, and blessing us with your spirit and handing over to us the very gift of life itself. You walked by our side in the garden and in the desert, over thorny ground and through green pastures. You who neither slumbers nor sleeps, you have been our keeper, never leaving us alone. It is you who keeps our going out and our coming in, from this day forth and even from the beginning of time to the end of all forevermores.

You are our God, marvelous and mysterious, steadfast and secure, and we, we are your children, playing hide and seek, running over hills and behind trees, hiding under branches and around fences—and we, we are your children, God, playing hide and seek, hiding behind old grudges, useless guilt, ancient and unproductive self-images, worn-out mind-sets . . . we are children puffed up with our own importance, impressed by our successes, protective of our "birth-rights" . . . running from responsibility, running from the pain of our brothers, the injustice to our sisters, running from world concerns and local problems, running away from you, God. And we, God, we are your children playing hide and seek, knowing in one part of us that you have already found us, and in another part, hoping to be found again, knowing that you have already freed us from our own bondage, our own efforts to hide, and hoping, hoping to hear you call again, "All ye, all ye, in come free." Tap us, again, precious God, and call out that we are yours, that we are found, that our games need no longer be played.

Touch us, O God, and tell us that we are it! Show us the way to help you find the hiding and lost ones. Instruct us in the ways of righteousness and peace. Uncloud our vision, break into our persistent privacy, and connect us to community. Pull us in the ways of partnership with all people that the realm of your hopes and dreams may flourish in your land, a new heaven and a new earth, yours and ours, by grace and works.

—Ann G. Abernethy
Wellesley, Massachusetts

Times of Trouble

Along the Rough Spots

My Cup Runneth Over

A Trying Day

Death Can Be Beautiful

Silence Is Not Emptiness

ALONG THE ROUGH SPOTS

Dear God,
Such a drastic change I'm dealing with
Please help me along the rough spots
   I know there will be many.
Sometimes I don't know what to do
   I don't know many answers.
I want to help her, but I can't
   the problem is too much for me.
Too much for me—that doesn't feel very good.
I always thought I could help people
   now I'm the one who needs help.
God, you are the only one who makes me feel better.
Mom and Dad have been great
   they try to understand
   they talk my feelings out with me.
But they are human like me
   they don't know all the answers.
You know the whole situation
   thanks for understanding
   thanks for always being there.
I can always count on you without exception.
Knowing that gives me comfort
   the problem doesn't disappear
   but the pain is lessened.
I kind of feel lucky to have you
   as if no one else does.

You seem to give me full attention
    I know you do to everyone.
I can't comprehend that
    but that's why I'm me and you're God.
I feel like people always come to me for help
    you must really think people do that to you.
I wish I talked to you more often
    I always seem to ask you for help or guidance.
    I wish I'd remember to talk to you when things
        are going great.
I have had a lot of great times in my life, you know
    just lately the bad times seem to stand out.
I've never had my mind challenged so much
    partly in school work
    but also many questions are coming to me.
Why do so many people have problems?
    but they do seem to solve them eventually.
I know I will too—of course I'll be faced with
    more in the future.
Dilemmas are part of life—what would it be like
    if everything were perfect—boring!
I'll make it—so will she
    we have to—we must.
I know you'll always be there for me.
It's nice to have at least one constant in my life.
Thanks. I love you.

—Lori S. Miller (at age 18)
Princeton Junction, New Jersey

MY CUP RUNNETH OVER

May I have your attention as I tell my tale of woe?
I was in a melancholy mood, feeling awfully low;
My burdens seemed so heavy, like more than I could bear;
The world drooped on my shoulders; I was filled with
   deep despair.
I could neither eat, nor sleep; I had no peace of mind;
The debts were piling up, and our payments way behind.
My children were provoking; everything was going
   wrong;
The days were dark, and nights seemed short instead of
   long.
My head ached constantly; that was indeed a bad sign.
I had to be careful, beware, or I'd cross the borderline.

The Spirit seemed to ask me, "Have you no faith in God?"
"Yes, oh yes!" I said aloud, and my head I did nod.
"Don't you believe what you tell others, in everything
   you write?
Then how could you say that your day seemed like the
   night?
Are you composing just to give people a lift?
If you have so little faith, I will have to take your gift!"
I wept, sang, and prayed, "God, forgive me if you can.
At times this world is so hard for all children.
Trust and faith I do have, if at times it seems to shatter.

Well, O God, I'm just human, and I guess that's what's
the matter.

"But then you knew all things long before I could even
walk.
I didn't want to tell you, but it's so much nicer when we
talk.
You were here through Jesus Christ and they crucified
you.
I'm trying to bear my cross, but I am weak, it's true.
I know that you are real, 'cause I feel better already.
If I should ever slip again, guide and keep me steady!
I love, thank, and need thee; protect me from strife.
I pray someday to live with thee in the land of clover.
If thou wilt but grant me this, O God, my cup runneth
over."

—*Bernice Barnes*
Chicago, Illinois

A TRYING DAY

O God,
This has been a trying day;
a day filled with confusion
   and doubt
in the midst of love and care.
There's such a thin line, dear God,
between being assertive
   and being selfish
and I've not yet learned to walk that line.
Help me to keep my balance, God,
and please pick me up when I fall.

O God, we're so lucky here.
May we not ignore the curses
and not dismiss the blessings.

Thank you for friends who love us enough
to challenge us to look inside
even as we grow
and reach out to you.
Amen.

—*Jeanne Lischer*
New Brighton, Minnesota

DEATH CAN BE BEAUTIFUL

Dear God,

Death can be beautiful.

Some people will say that I am morbid for making a statement of this sort. I have been touched by many personal deaths and feel that I am qualified to make these remarks. My paternal grandmother and her mother (my great-grandmother) lived together for many years. My grandmother was an only child, but the mother of fourteen children. The year that I was fifteen is the time I remember them best; the year they both died.

My grandmother was called "Big Mama" because she was fat. We called her mother "Little Grandma" because she was thin and to distinguish between them. Big Mama was in her 70s, and Little Grandma was a hundred-odd years old. Little Grandma was blind from age but was very active. She would visit with her grandchildren for weeks at a time, but the moment she thought something was wrong with her daughter, she would return home. She was always concerned about her daughter and didn't want anything to happen to her when she wasn't there.

Death came one day to Big Mama and Little Grandma was in the house when the ambulance came to take Big

Mama away. Little Grandma didn't utter a word. She had a trunk that she never let anyone near. After Big Mama was taken away, Little Grandma gave up the key to her trunk, went to bed and died. She departed this life five hours after her daughter died.

Many times she had stated verbally that without her daughter she would have no reason for living. She had made her peace with you, O God, and her request was granted.

I can remember the minister's words as he was eulogizing this mother and daughter. The daughter saying, "Good-bye," but the mother saying, "Wait for me."

"God promised never to leave us alone."

Death was beautiful.

—*Luesther Chapman*
Chicago, Illinois

SILENCE IS NOT EMPTINESS

Is this the place called Gethsemane—the place of soli-
tude—the hill of fervent prayer?
Is this the time called betrayal—of desertion and darkness
and fear?
Is this the moment of crucifixion—of future dashed—of
hope dying—of pain and grief?

In my prayers I cry out to you, O Holy One.
In my time of need, I seek your promise of love.

Reassure me with your words—
    Hope is never abandoned . . .
        Light is not extinguished . . .
            Silence is not emptiness . . .

Your love for me, O God, is like the deepness of a well.
    As a well is filled by minute sources, each adding to
        the whole,
        so too am I filled—
            by memories of love,
                by shared celebration,
                    by collected vision and dreams.
    As a well echoes in its depth,
        so too your love resounds in me—
            in the gentleness of a friend,

in the glimpse of a loved one,
in the strength of a friend.

The well renews itself by its very use.
The drawn water encourages more water to take its
place.
May I share your love in that renewal . . .
May my actions encourage another to action.
May my words be the lamp to another's footsteps.
May my silence join another's, and
May your voice be heard.

Silence is not emptiness. Gethsemane is no longer dark.
Your life is in me, O Holy One.

Amen.

—*Nancy Nelson Elsenheimer*
Poughkeepsie, New York

One in the Spirit

Trinity

Fellowship Prayer

United in Faith

Blessings and Guidance

Meal Blessing

TRINITY

Father of all mercy
Mother of all comfort
You are one . . . one in the Spirit . . . one in the Christ . . .
One within the Trinity!

I seek thee. Open to me
That I may know your acceptance
That I may hear your approval . . .

Acceptance of my sinfulness
Approval of my freedom from it.

As I grow closer to you through Christ
Who is and was and shall be all in all,
I am so grateful for our future hope:
    a place in your household
    a room of my own
    a connecting door to all those the Spirit has taught me
        to love.

Soon I shall be close enough to knock . . .
To see your smile and hear joy,
Though tears, pain, and the shadow of death yet trouble
    us.
I ask for release from the pain, a tender touch to wipe

away the tears, and through the Christ, who with the Spirit
keeps me seeking, I know that release shall be and that touch transforms. Death shall trouble us no more.

Then we shall be one . . . all we whom the Spirit has gathered . . .
All we who have been kept from captivity by the truth of God's love . . .
All we who have heard Jesus' word of forgiveness and call to unity.

Most holy God, I thank you for the water of life you give without cost.
My thirst for it and my baptism in it has brought me your mercy and
comfort and revealed your great capacity for caring for the world.

Yet I wait for the final affirmation . . . the most precious gift . . .
your affirmation of my origin with you . . . for before you I am yet
a child . . . like every other child . . . like every other one.
All of us are one before you . . . longing to receive recognition that we are in your will . . . the one will of God.

All we offer is ourselves . . . our separate individual selves . . .
that you may unite us in your parental embrace in the whole household of your love. *Amen!*

—*Doris Judy*
De Soto, Missouri

FELLOWSHIP PRAYER

Help us to live together as people of one family, God, caring for others' needs and concerns more than our own. Help us to be gentle, walking softly with one another. Help us to be understanding and not condemning till we have tried walking in one another's shoes. Help us to be as eager to forgive others as we are to seek forgiveness. Help us to know no barriers of creed or race, that our love may be like thine—a love that sees all men and women of all nations on earth as thy children and our brothers and sisters.

We ask these prayers in the name of our church family. May thy blessing be on each one of us now and forever more. *Amen.*

—Eileen Stock
Storrs, Connecticut

UNITED IN FAITH

Our creator God, we join together in our prayer for the many voices that are raised to you, raised in the longings that are felt, in the joys that are expressed, and in the concerns that we all have, not only here in our immediate midst, but for all who are in need of loving care.

We pray for all who in their diversity are still united in their faith. Help us to be seekers of vision, knowing that if we will be open to your call for service, you will be with us and give us the strength and wisdom to carry out your will.

All this we pray in Jesus' name. *Amen.*

—Irene Graessle
Maplewood, New Jersey

BLESSINGS AND GUIDANCE

Almighty God, whose power
    and love are
    forever,
pour down blessings and
    guidance for
    your people,
for churches where our God
    is worshiped
in the love and truth that
    Jesus gave us.
Grant all pastors that
    Holy Spirit,
your gift to humankind.
Fill the hearts of the faithful
    with the
    everlasting power of the
    Almighty.
This prayer pours out through
    the Holy Spirit
in the name of our Jesus Christ.

Amen.

—*Gladyce W. De Jonge*
San Diego, California

MEAL BLESSING

LEADER: God of the earth,
God of all humanity,
We join hands to bless this food;
We join hands to bless one another.

We thank you for the hands that have prepared this meal: shopping, washing, cutting, chopping, stirring, arranging, baking . . . in this home and outside this home.

PEOPLE: **Bless these hands; we are one circle.**

LEADER: We thank you for the hands that have grown and brought us this food: tilling, planting, picking, milking, processing, counting, wrapping, carrying . . . in nearby fields and factories and in fields and factories far away.

PEOPLE: **Bless these hands; we are one circle.**

LEADER: We thank you for the hands of our circle that join together in thanksgiving. We cry out to you for the empty hands that plead for mercy, for food, for rest, for employment.

PEOPLE: **Bless these hands; we are one circle.**

LEADER: God of the earth,
God of all humanity,
Teach us that we are one circle;

Bless this food that we may see it as a sign of our interdependence
And as a call to use these hands of ours, blessed by this community and this food, so that all may have bread.

ALL: *Amen.*

—Christina J. Del Piero
Middlebury, Vermont
(written in Brazil)

Open to Nurture

Life Is So Daily

For a Home of Happy Memories

To Warm Another's Heart

LIFE IS SO DAILY

Life is so daily, O God, and somehow the days go faster now.

Help me to remember
  to be thankful that they do go fast,
  that there are the letters to write to the children and grandchildren, and prayers to be said in their behalf,
  that the phone calls and visits to the shut-ins need to be made,
  that the leaders in our groups need to be complimented and encouraged to try new things,
  that I need to listen compassionately to the cares and concerns of others,
  that I am healthy, have a husband to provide a home, meals, and clean clothes for, to encourage and inspire and take a day off with,
  that I have a heritage that has instilled in me qualities of caring, leadership, and responsibility.

Keep challenging me, O God, to what more I can do during my stay here on this earth. In Jesus' name, *Amen.*
                                        —*Betty J. Kemper*
                                        Omaha, Nebraska

FOR A HOME OF HAPPY MEMORIES

Dear God, help me to make our home a place of happy memories.

I pray that in years to come our children and grandchildren will remember with pleasure
> the smell of homemade hot bread and rolls, the taste of homemade strawberry jam, hot cookies, and milk after school,
> the Thanksgiving, Christmas, and Easter celebrations with family members, relatives, and friends,
> the family reunions every summer,
> the birthday parties throughout the year,
> the special love for playful kittens and puppies,
> the loving thoughts our children put into words when they were tucked in bed.

I thank thee, O God, for the happy experiences with our children and grandchildren. Keep me, I pray, sensitive to their needs and ever ready to listen when they wish to talk, and enable me to give them all my love and many blessings.

I pray in Christ's name. *Amen.*

—Irene Sick
Perkinsville, New York

TO WARM ANOTHER'S HEART

I am God's channel
For inspiring deeds and positive action.

My life reflects this,
And the glow is seen by all those around me.

May that glow warm another's heart
And help her lead a serene existence.

—Pat Hutson
Chicago, Illinois

Called to Serve

My Sisters

Love Begins with Us

Trustees of the Future

Servants for Justice and Peace

Task for Thy Glory

Go Forth in Mission

Eyes to See

Our Prayer

MY SISTERS

Our tasks are undone . . . and there's no time to rest!
Our strivings increase . . . yet we fear every test!
Nobody even knows our names, let alone when we've
    done our best!

Our lives make so little sense;
We're vulnerable
Without defense.

Oh, it's not just happening to us, we know.
We look around . . . the whole world's a mess.
Too many wars; too much distress.

No rationale . . . no love; just pain and dismay!
O God, bow down and hear our prayer;
In thy blessed presence let us stay . . . to know thy truth
    anew.

There is no task too great or small
When to thee we surrender all.
Noways tired we'll be . . . when on thy everlasting arms
    we lean.

Bless us by your presence, God;
Set our minds aglow
So abundant lives we'll know.

44

Let our eyes see thy glory in the dawning of each day;
Let our ears hear thy voice
Tenderly calling all the way.

Let our hearts be filled to overflowing
Caring, sharing, doing, knowing
More love to thee and one another.

Bless our minds to be stayed on thee;
Let us live and move, and in thy blessed presence be
Forever and ever!

—Barbara J. Allen
Chicago, Illinois

LOVE BEGINS WITH US

It's Advent!
O God, we are waiting again
Standing on tiptoe with expectancy and hope.
We're waiting for . . . we don't know what . . .
Surprise, wonder, something different
Maybe even change in our lives.
At least, change in our circumstances.

Strange isn't it?
That a date on a calendar
That isn't even *the* birthday
Should suddenly raise our expectations.
Absurd really, for he is already here, waiting
Waiting for us to discover him again
Waiting for us to celebrate love again
To experience peace in our hearts and in our world
Waiting for us to be reconciled
To him, to one another.

It's Advent!
O God, help us to stop waiting and
Get on with the celebration
At home and at work.
In New York City and New Jersey,
Connecticut and the world.

Comfort . . . .*
Sustain . . . .
Bring healing to . . . .

Love begins with us, O God.
Peace was part of the shepherds' promise.
We *know* that. We *do* know that.
So help us get off hold,
Stop waiting, and live love now!
Amen.

—*Beverly J. Chain*
New York, New York

*Note: Complete these sentences with your own specialized concerns and issues and people in your group.

TRUSTEES OF THE FUTURE

Eternal God, we thank you for all the blessings that you so richly bestow on us. We thank you for life itself. Grant that we may ever be grateful and that we continue a spirit of good will toward one another and all people. We are thankful for your promise that where two or three are gathered in your name you are present.

We dedicate to you the thoughts of our minds, the loyalty of our hearts, and the serving of our hands.

Help us, we pray, to work toward the bettering of life for all people. May we be aware that we occupy a space to cherish and then pass on to someone else. May we realize that we are stewards of your land, responsible for its beauty and use.

Help us to break free from thinking of only our own selves and our group. We are the trustees of the future. We must think beyond ourselves. We must consider the effects our acts and decisions will have on those who come after us.

Amen.

—Irene Stock
Honeoye Falls, New York

SERVANTS FOR JUSTICE AND PEACE

Thank you, Eternal Friend, for the wide, wonderful universe that you have created; for all the manner of living creatures and life forms; and for each of us.

Please help us to discover the finely tuned balance and harmony you have established between the ecosystems.

We acknowledge our blindness, ingratitude, and greed. Save us from the lust for pleasure, profit, power, and privilege.

Guide us, we pray, until we realize our own importance and interdependence. Help us to admit that we need to respect you, ourselves, and one another.

May we discover that cooperation is more fruitful than competition.

We would be good stewards of your resources and not waste them on instruments of death and destruction.

For all the hurts we have inflicted and sustained, forgive us.

Teach us to pray, to lay down our burdens of anger and resentment and forgive with all our hearts.

We are grateful that in your undying love, you have promised, to all who believe in you, the comfort and presence of your Holy Spirit.

Compassionate Creator, who has made each of us unique, teach us to pray, to accept our own and others' uniqueness with joy. With your help, may we use our specialness to enrich life on earth and be your servants for Justice and Peace.

Amen.

—*Evelyn S. Murray*
Portland, Oregon

TASK FOR THY GLORY

Our God in heaven, help us to love one another more perfectly and may everything we say and do here today contribute to a community of faith and to an increase in love and loyalty. Give us some worthwhile task to do for thy glory and the ability to do it worthily. Give us the spirit of sincere gratitude for all who have done their work conscientiously. Give us the quiet satisfaction which comes with the knowledge that we have done our best. *Amen.*

—Harriet Gadway
Omaha, Nebraska

GO FORTH IN MISSION

O holy God, we know that we are gathered in your name
(tonight) because you came looking for us. You called
us to this place. We have been led to you by other people who, while loving you, have told others so that they,
too, could enjoy knowing you.

Eternal and everlasting God, modern skills and technolo-
gy have made neighbors of your children whom we used
to think lived in distant places of the earth. Help us to
know in our hearts that we cannot fully enjoy the good
products of today if all our neighbors cannot enjoy them
also. We are not safe from harmful products of modern
times if others are not safe also.

Dear Savior and Redeemer, we confess to you that we
have not tried very hard to get to know our neighbors
on this earth. We really do not know if they are hungry,
cold, or too hot—if they hurt, are sorrowful or ill. We
do know that they hunger for the Bread of Life that only
you can provide. We pray that you will lead us to take
Christian responsibility in these matters. You do not ask
us to "take charge." You are so wonderfully and marvel-
ously "in charge." Often, you do not ask us to do the
big jobs. But if we go from this place *(tonight)* and continue to talk with you, you will lead us to know the little

things we can do. And if we will do these little things in your name, you will weave them into the fabric of your plan and purpose for all your children on this planet.

Gracious God, your love is here *(tonight)*. It comes from you and touches each person here. It is a connecting link from each of us to every other person here. And we can share your love with all people we meet and with those we know are out there in your world. We pray that you will lead us to join with Christian people everywhere in loving, sharing, and caring on this earth. We ask these things in the precious name of Jesus, our Lord.

Amen.

—*Ruth Cooper*
Creve Coeur, Missouri

EYES TO SEE

Dear God: Give me eyes to see the work you would have me do. Give me ears to hear the need of others, lips to speak of your love that brings peace and comfort to those in need, a heart to love and bring joy to those in pain and trouble, hands to do the simple task for you and others, loving the unlovable. Help me and guide me every day to live and spread happiness to others. I ask in your name. *Amen.*

—Goldie Bleir
Council Grove, Kansas

OUR PRAYER

Our heavenly Creator, as we renew ourselves in our purpose not only as women of this church, but also as persons working for the total growth and welfare of the church universal,

Help us as we *comfort* the sick and lonely, the shut-ins and the elderly;

Help us to *promote* goodwill and friendliness throughout your church;

Help us to *give* of ourselves through the gifts and talents you have so freely given us;

Help us to *love* and *understand* people of other faiths and nationalities;

Help us to be true *witnesses* of your son, Jesus, through daily living in our homes, community, and this world;

Help us as we *support* those in the missionary field both spiritually and materially and help them to know that we care;

Help us to *understand* one another as we work together, to put aside personal gain and recognition, to put aside human jealousies that so often cause hurt and misunderstandings;

Help us through *patience*, through *forgiveness*, always to work together for unity.

For all these things, dear heavenly God, we ask your guidance and your strength. Hear us now as in our hearts we thank you for these things and all our many other blessings, through Jesus, your son, the living Christ. *Amen.*

—*Gloria Christman*
East Greenville, Pennsylvania

Open to Change

Called and Free

Let Us Pray for Faith

New Awareness

CALLED AND FREE

O God, we have given you thanks for creating us to be women of your spirit.
We give you thanks that you have called us and freed us through the life, death, and resurrection of Jesus Christ.
Pour out your spirit on all who have come together this day, your daughters and your sons.
Bless us as we move through these next few days. As you blessed those gathered at Pentecost, bless us now.
By the power of your spirit, let us see clearly where you would have us go.
Let us hear the cries for liberation and justice that come from the lips and lives of the oppressed, our sisters and brothers all over your world.
By the power of your spirit, let us be your prophetic voices in this modern-day wilderness.
Let us dream the impossible dreams, being ever mindful that all things are possible through you.
By the power of your spirit, enable us to be ministers of healing, reconciliation, and wholeness.
O God of our mothers and grandmothers,
O God of Sarah, Miriam, and Esther,
O God of Sojourner, Antoinette, and Teresa,
As pieces of fabric, weave us together in new patterns.
Use our differences to quilt together new designs of movement toward the coming of your reign on earth.

Weave the fabric of our lives as women in the spirit called and free.
Through Jesus Christ, we pray.
Amen and *amen*.

—*Second National Meeting
of United Church of Christ Women*

LET US PRAY FOR FAITH

Thoughts of childhood bring back images of the beginnings of faith, sweet and uncomplicated. But life does not turn out to be sweet and uncomplicated. The path each of us must follow is not always easy. We must walk our path in faith. We must follow in faith; we must speak with faith!

Now, let us pray for faith . . .

. . . for faith that supports and sustains when we must make choices that are complex and difficult; faith that is more than simplistic answers to life's most difficult choices.

(Pause for silent prayer)

. . . for faith that is growing and lively, open to new truth, but grounded in ancient wisdom; faith that matures as we mature.

(Pause for silent prayer)

. . . for faith that is strong enough to respect the beliefs of others, and that does not crumble in the face of prejudice and hatred.

(Pause for silent prayer)

. . . for faith that burns with intensity for justice, and still sustains us when justice calls for sacrifice.

(Pause for silent prayer)

. . . for faith that gives us the words we must speak when we can no longer be silent.

(Pause for silent prayer)

. . . for faith that compels us to acts of kindness and compassion, not vindictiveness and malice.

(Pause for silent prayer)

. . . for faith that acknowledges our ambiguity, but will not let us go.

(Pause for silent prayer)

. . . for faith that moves and inspires others, expressed in words, and law, and acts which show compassion, wisdom, and justice.

(Pause for silent prayer)

God, we accept your gracious gift of faith in all its mystery, power, and joy, that we might know you more deeply and intensely every day that we live. *Amen.*

—Marilyn M. Breitling
A bidding prayer from the interfaith service,
First Congregational UCC, Washington, D.C.,
March for Women's Lives, March 9, 1986

NEW AWARENESS

LEADER: Here, God, we are yours. Silent now, but filled with new awareness of all our possibilities. Still now, yet full of energy for the bringing of your reign of justice. Prayerfully we come to hear your word and celebrate the gospel that makes us the new beings we are only just discovering inside ourselves. With hope we approach you in worship that we may celebrate the community we have become.

Great and gracious God, we have known your presence in our midst through calls to personhood, to faith and to action. We turn humbly in confession to acknowledge that we have failed you and one another and ourselves.

VOICE I: O God our Creator, we confess that we have turned away from the startling reality of our creation in your image. Out of fear, we have turned our backs on the dominion granted us at the beginning of time and accepted cultural definitions of femininity and masculinity. We recognize now that by these sins we have distorted your image on this earth. O merciful God,

62

	forgive us for failing to be with you the co-creators we were called to be.
PEOPLE:	**Forgive us and make us free!**
VOICE II:	O God of all wisdom, confronted by injustice and the awesome powers and principalities of our day, we recoil in fear and take refuge in our powerlessness. Frozen into passivity and hiding behind complexity, we pray for others to take action at moments when our leadership is necessary. O merciful God, forgive us for forgetting that your Spirit brings wisdom and power to those who must step forward at times like these.
PEOPLE:	**Forgive us and make us bold!**
VOICE III:	O God of all the universe, we confess that we have permitted the happenstance of birth to divide us not only from, but also against one another. We celebrate our differences and yet we fail to create that unity which the gospel demands. O merciful God, forgive us for not keeping ourselves open to your Spirit, which unites and empowers us for mission.
PEOPLE:	**Forgive us and make us one!**
VOICE IV:	O God of all time, forgive us. We live in a society that wastes resources and people. We have become used to such waste, and to believing that only the young and the new and the shiny have value. We are a people of obsolescence. Yet you are a God of tradition who promises to make all things new. O merciful God, forgive us for

our willingness to be every kind of new creation but yours.

PEOPLE: **Forgive us and make us new!**

LEADER: Come closer, God, and hear the inner yearnings of these your people who seek to be faithful, who long to live justly and to live for justice. We seek your loving forgiveness as assuredly as we are a people of faith. For in this prayer, we confess not only our wrongdoing, but also our faith. Come God our creator, who is Jesus the Christ. Come through your Holy Spirit and free us of these burdens.

PEOPLE: *Amen!*

—First National Meeting
of United Church of Christ Women

Strength in the Struggle

Ring of Possibility

Show Us the Way

Lament of the Homeless Woman

Dare to Intercede

Recall Your Vision

One Tapestry

The Prayer of a Minister's Wife

RING OF POSSIBILITY

Comforter God, soft mantle of life, wrap us in love.

Knit us into that cloud of witnesses,
   that long scarf of time with
     stripe
       after
         stripe
         of stories of bravery and boldness.

By those stripes we are healed.
  By Ruth's journey and
    Deborah's wisdom and
      Rhoda's persistence,
        and Mary's grieving.

By those stories we are knitted into an ongoing journey.

  Moses hearing "how many more miles?"
    from the back seat of his caravan.
  Abraham, tearless, fearless,
    over his son on bundled sticks.
  Jesus, faithful even to the pain of
    the cross.

O God, give us strength! Make our circle
   a yoke of service,
      a flotation collar of hope,
         a muffler against the winds of war,
            a ring of possibility, in Christ's name.
            Amen.

—*Laura Loving*
Minneapolis, Minnesota

Reprinted by permission of the United Church of Christ Office for Church Life and Leadership.

SHOW US THE WAY

Dear God,

What are we doing, we your people? Why are we killing and maiming and destroying one another?

We show great compassion for the unborn and yet manufacture weapons and teach our youth how to use them against the precious living.

We fear one another to the point of hate so strong that we are willing to annihilate those who oppose our ideals.

Will the common people never have the thinking power, love, and strength to say "enough, we will no longer fight our world family for any reason"?

We would rather help those who need help and try to make living a joy and the pleasant experience we are sure you, our God, meant it to be for everyone.

Please, dear God, countenance our bad and foolish behavior no longer. Show us all the way to thy kingdom.
Amen.

—Grace Losi
Lockport, New York

LAMENT OF THE HOMELESS WOMAN

O Mary, mother of Jesus,
  I cry to you because
  you alone can understand me.

I am weary and worn,
  tired of carrying my bags from door to door,
  tired of having to move on,
  tired of having no place to call my own.

No one seems to understand
  how or why I came this way.
Even I do not fully know.
  I was confused and alone
  without friends who cared.

The hospital workers said I could go home,
  but where was I to go, what was I to do?

My family only laughed when I returned.
  They had no room, no time, no place for me,
  with my fears and anxieties.

There are voices that haunt me,
  until I have no peace.
  So I just move on, move on, move on.

Where will it end?
  Where will I go?

Mary, mother of Jesus,
  I come to you
  with my sadness, my woe—
  You will hear my cry,
  You will understand.
                    Amen.

—*Geneva M. Butz*
Philadelphia, Pennsylvania

DARE TO INTERCEDE

O God of the helpless and hopeless,
  Hear me: I want to pray.
  I want to pray for those who are desperate
    and despairing, wretched and forsaken.
  I want to pray for those who, exhausted by
    the struggle against oppression, are
    unable to pray for themselves.
  (But I am afraid . . .)

Hear the cries of those who are in
anguish. Heal their wounds. Nourish
them in their hunger. Comfort them
in their need. Give them strength
and endurance in the struggle. Give
them hope in the future.

O God of love,
  Help me: How can I intercede for them?
  How *dare* I intercede for them—I who
    have known no hunger or thirst, no
    homelessness or brutality, no abuse
    or alienation from my loved ones?
  (. . . am afraid that if I intercede through
  prayer, I am called to intercede through
  action.)

Help your children. Send your Holy
Spirit to them when they are too
weak to call forth your power in
their own behalf.

O God of life,
   Enliven me: so that I am less wary of life.
   Teach me: to understand lives that I may
      never live.
   Enable me: to weep for others as I am
      sometimes able to weep for myself.
   Open me: to receive the pouring out of
      your spirit.
   (I am still afraid, but not so much. Your
   presence changes my prayer, . . . changes
   me!)

Let your life-giving spirit empower
me so that I may act to transform the
lives of your suffering children. Open
my eyes that I may see ways to meet
their needs. Enable me to confront and
change the wicked world that so
desolates and oppresses them. I ask
it in the name of the one who brings
new life to all, Jesus the Christ.
      Amen.   *Amen.*

—*Betsie G. Tremant*
Houston, Texas

RECALL YOUR VISION

Our God, and God of all the world's peoples, known by many names, creator of this wondrous universe: we come into your presence to recall once again your vision for us while we search earnestly for your truth for this day in the life of this church. We praise you, O God, for your many good gifts to us:
For life,
For the beauty and bounty of your world,
For the infinite variety of your human family.
For the gift of human companionship by which our lives are linked in common aspiration. We celebrate your spirit poured out on us in every endeavor of our lives.

We ask your forgiveness for those times when we have closed our hearts to the prompting of your Holy Spirit and narrowed our horizons to what is comfortable and safe. We ask your forgiveness for the violence around us and within us, and for all the occasions when we have failed to speak for justice and peace. Forgive us, O God, for the times when your word and your will remained mute in us, for our failure to be fully alive to our potential, for failure to risk courageously.

God, our Sustainer and our Redeemer, we thank you for this church, for leaders and followers today, and for those who have gone before us to serve your world as teachers and preachers, missionaries and healers, men and women, faith-filled and committed who carried your message of hope, reconciliation, and redemption around the world so that today we are partners with those we may never know but in whose kinship we are bound as sisters and brothers in Christ.

As we struggle to know your will in regard to the grave issues facing the church and the world, grant to us the grace to see that another's truth may not be our truth but that both of us may be motivated by the same search for light. Make us gentle and loving and forgiving with each other as we fashion a path for this church in the years ahead. Keep us sensitive to our rich heritage, but let us not be immobilized by a past in which we no longer live. May the God who is always with us fill that which is empty in us, complete that which is incomplete, mold with care that which is poorly formed, bring to life the courage that falters and through Christ, our Redeemer, redirect our lives. Move us beyond stirring words to deeds that reveal to the world whose we are and in whose image we try to live. As we return to homes across the world, keep before us your vision of a world in which every person is treasured, in which power is used responsibly, in which life is lived sensitively with respect to our fragile, finite planet. Open our eyes and our hearts to serve others in their need wherever that need exists.

In that service may our lives truly reflect the one in whose footsteps we follow, Jesus the Christ, in whose name we pray. *Amen.*

—Harriet McGeehan
West Hazleton, Pennsylvania

ONE TAPESTRY

To you we lift our praise,
"Our God, our help in ages past, our hope for years to come, our shelter from the stormy blast and our eternal home."* Ever aware of the slow but definite ticking of the clock, the ticking away of our lives, we come before the One who is eternal, to whom "a thousand ages . . . are like an evening gone."*

We come before you, dear God, a little bent, a little weary. We are merely human, O Holy One, and we have seen too much already it sometimes seems. Too much of hunger, too much of poverty, too much of death, too much of strife between nations. We are wearing thin around the heart. We must either build a new and stronger wall around our hearts or risk being mortally wounded. Or so it seems. Yet one more time we will struggle to put aside our concern with ourselves and lift to you our prayers for the needy of the earth; the homeless in Lebanon and Los Angeles; the parentless children of Bombay; the persecuted in Siberia and Santiago; the lonely and wandering on land and at sea; the suffering and the mourning in every huddled mass of people throughout the world.

*From a hymn by Isaac Watts, based on Psalm 90.

We pray your blessing, your touch, your loving hand to rest on them. And on us. We need you; we need one another. You have bound us together with the thread of creation. We are one tapestry, woven, sewn, embroidered by your fingers. Let our designs reflect your glory. Let our patterns blend harmoniously into the whole, yet free to dance our own designs.

Let us see beyond our daily struggles, our pain, our loneliness, our searching, our need, to the wonder and beauty of which we are a part. You have created us in love to live in love—with you—with all humanity—with all the earth. Teach us your way of love as revealed to us in the way of Jesus of Nazareth, in whose name we pray. *Amen.*

—*Mary Sue Gast*
Indianapolis, Indiana

THE PRAYER OF A MINISTER'S WIFE

Are you listening, God? I mean *really* listening? Not just hearing me like people do, with their ears only, but with your heart and mind? I don't want advice, judgment, not even agreement. I just want to be listened to—and understood because—'though I speak with the tongue of a minister's wife and understand all people and have all knowledge of the church (according to the parish), I am still a person in my own right. I think—I feel—I act as a person. I understand and want to be understood and accepted as a person. But I can be more than I am. I know because in my highest moments I achieve that goal.

I can't exactly remember having chosen to be a minister's wife as a vocation, but I *can* remember choosing the wife part of it, falling in love with a dreamy-eyed young theologue with little thought at the time, I suspect, of sharing that dream as helpmeet, hostess, and Holy Ghostess to the whole parish.

Why does the world eye me a little askance—and yet a little hopefully? Why am I expected to do what others can't (or won't) "because you are the minister's wife"? Do they think we, as a breed apart, acquire a certain osmosis through marriage to a servant of God not granted to others? An automatic plug-in to perfection perhaps? A hot line to God, as it were, granted only to the Mistress of the Manse?

Forgive me, God. I don't mean to be frivolous or cynical because I *am* proud to be a member of the firm: God-My Husband-Me-Inc. But I do feel that Paul anticipated the minister's wife's needs when he listed the gifts of the spirit: love, joy, peace, patience, kindness, goodness, faithfulness, gentleness, and self-control. A sense of humor helps, too, because there *are* frustrations:

criticism of me—if I take an active part in church affairs, I am accused of "running things." If I stand by and wait to be asked, I am "failing to support my husband."

criticism of my children—they are "wild and undisciplined" if they behave like those of the parish families, or they are "repressed" and "square" to their peers if they fail to go along with the crowd.

criticism of my husband—he is "too liberal" for some of the congregation and "too conservative" for the rest. "How dare he speak out on controversial issues?" or else "He is retreating to the sanctimonious safety of the Bible when he should be speaking to the issues of the day!"

At such times *I* am *his* minister, his confidant, his listener—a privilege to be welcomed with open heart, hands, and ears and not abused with open mouth.

There are jealousies, too—of his time—what wouldn't I give sometimes for an 8-to-5, five-days-a-week job with family time on Sunday, at least *one* evening a week free of board and committee meetings; a meal uninterrupted by a phone call; an emergency not taking precedence over a promised outing.

jealousy of hard-earned treasure: a new outfit purchased at sacrifice sets off the whispered comments: "How can she afford *that* on his salary?" or if year before last's is made to do, it's "Why is she so shabby? You'd think she'd consider her husband's position!" And always there are the "causes" for which we must set a good example through our giving, although modernizing the parsonage kitchen is *not* a luxury in which the property committee can indulge this year.

But when I stand at his side in the narthex, see the gratefulness shine from the eyes of a comforted widow, a reconciled couple, a repentant youth; hear a word of encouragement for a difficult stand taken, a hand clasp because of an effective sermon over which he has labored long, praise for his support of a controversial issue; when I feel the "warmth of belonging" that comes from needing and being needed by a parish, the privilege of being thought worthy to serve your humanity, the respect and recognition I share in the community as "The Minister's Wife"; catch the silent signal across a crowded room that means: "Among all these people I need and love YOU"—then it is I take extra pride in ironing the white shirts, darning the black socks, stretching the meat loaf and clothing budget, and I thank you for the privilege of serving with *your* servant.

So please, God, give me patience, an understanding heart, the quick discernment of soul to see another's need, the courage when wounded to stand, awareness of my weaknesses as well as my strengths, and the wisdom to use the "holy no" when it will benefit myself and others more than saying "yes" because "it's the thing to do."

Help me to love more people and to love them more and at the same time to leave myself open to the love and criticism of others; willing to take risks; to create an atmosphere of which others may be aware and in which they may be themselves. Help me to cultivate a sense of what is beyond my sight and rise above my complaisant self that I may truly be as Eve was to Adam, a helpmate for him with whom I am proud to serve. More than all these and in them all may I continue to strive to know you through your Son, to live a Christ-centric life instead of an ego-centric one.

Oh yes, and thanks for listening! *Amen.*

—Jean Giffin
Charlevoix, Michigan

Moments of Thanks

Open Our Hearts

Water of Life

Heard and Answered

OPEN OUR HEARTS

O gracious God of us all, we open our hearts to you this day in humble adoration and thanksgiving for all your kindness and forgiveness. As we approach you, we are mindful of the many needs of the women in our churches as they strive to do the work that they have planned.

The work of the women has come about by the devotion of many leaders who have labored tirelessly to bring to the attention of the churches how the women could aid in the Christian work. We ask thy blessing on these efforts and pray that thou wilt bless our leaders. We pray that all our groups will be drawn closer to thee and thou wilt be with each fellowship.

We thank thee for the many different gifts thou hast given that we can use in service to thee. And God, we thank thee for the Holy Spirit, who is our teacher and helper.

And now, O God, we ask thy forgiveness for the many times we have disappointed you by the things we have said and done that are displeasing to you.

We pray this in the name of our Lord and Savior, Jesus Christ.

Amen.

—*Emma F. Tibbets*
Rapid City, South Dakota

WATER OF LIFE

We thank you, Almighty God, for the gift of water. Over it the Holy Spirit moved in the beginning of creation. Through it you led the children of Israel out of their bondage in Egypt into the land of promise. In it your son, Jesus, received baptism and was anointed by the Holy Spirit as the Christ, to lead us, through his death and resurrection, from bondage to freedom, from darkness to light.

We thank you, loving God, for the water of life. It flows as your spirit to give us new birth. Now sanctify us, we pray, by the power of your Holy Spirit that, refreshed by the waters of faith, we might live toward a new day of justice and peace and carry healing waters to a dry and thirsty world.

Amen.

*—Second National Meeting
of United Church of Christ Women*

HEARD AND ANSWERED

Dear God, we thank thee for the great privilege of coming to thee with our joys and sorrows, our fears and anxieties—knowing that we shall be heard and answered.

Help us, O God, to pray aright. We are too prone to beseech thy blessings on ourselves and those we hold most dear, instead of remembering the cold, the hungry, the homeless, the unloved and the unlovely, the unchurched, the godless, who are also thy children.

We are thankful for our homes, for our families and our friends, whether they are absent or present with us. We ask for them thy loving care, encouragement, and strength.

May thy Spirit hover over our beloved country and all those in authority, for whom we humbly ask thy direct guidance and help.

Grant that we may greet each day with gladness and perform such tasks as come to us with cheerfulness and joy in thy name.

We ask all in the name of thy precious Son, our Lord and Savior, Jesus Christ. *Amen.*

—Marjorie B. Robbins
North Franklin, Connecticut

Sending Forth

As We Leave

Reflecting Your Word

AS WE LEAVE

And now as we leave this place,
Let us hold fast to our sacred visions.
Dare to take them to all of our ordinary places.
And then reach beyond toward a new, more inclusive
community.
As we believe, so we must care, and as we care, so we
must do.

For we are indeed called, we are free to become united
and whole.

—*Betsy Huntley*
Wellesley, Massachusetts

REFLECTING YOUR WORD

Almighty God, Creator of all things, the miniscule and the gigantic, the giver of every perfect gift, ruler over day and night, we come to you at the end of our time together and present to you at this time our thoughts and actions.

We pray earnestly that you will find them acceptable; that our discussions, deliberations, and decisions do truly reflect your Word. We come from diverse cultures, from various environments, and we have been influenced by unique families and have had tremendously varied life experiences. Yet we all share a marvelous and wonderful gift, your enduring, sustaining, nurturing, protecting, guiding love, as father and mother to each of us.

As we end our meeting, bless us, we pray, in that secret place deep within us which only you can know, where our closest and most precious thoughts dwell, dear memories languish, and great dreams begin. Purify us, rest us, so that tomorrow we may come with renewed vigor, and approach our tasks with creative thought, with attentiveness, open-mindedness, and humility.

We ask these things in the name of Jesus Christ, who is the Prince of Peace, the Lord of Love, and the Servant of Justice.

Amen.

—*Toyo Nakamura*
Honolulu, Hawaii